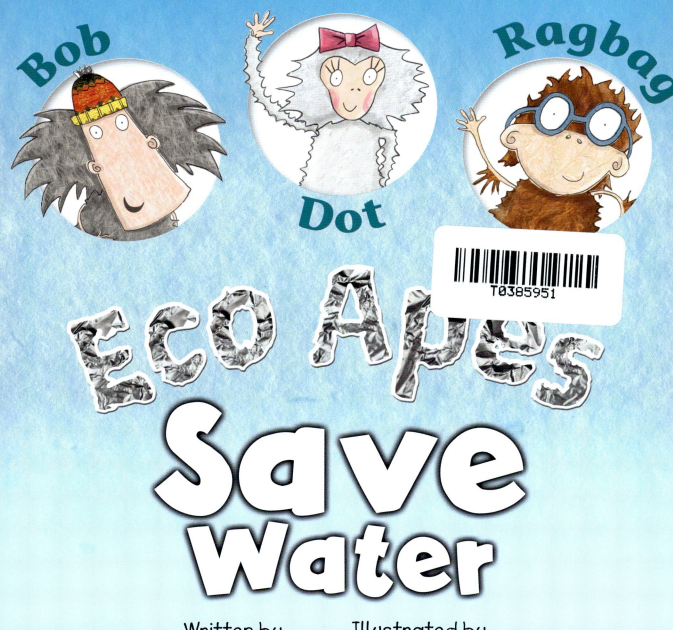

Bob

Dot

Ragbag

Eco Apes

Save
Water

Written by
Greg Cook

Illustrated by
Mark Chambers

"I can save water," said Bob.

"How?" said Dot.

"Look!" said Bob. "I will get
lots of water in this cup."

"No," said Ragbag. "That is no good."

"Look!" said Ragbag. "I will get lots of water in this hat."

"No," said Dot. "That is no good."

"Look!" said Dot. "We can get lots of water from the fish tank."

"No!" said Bob. "The fish
need that water!"

Bob got a big tub.

"Look!" said Bob. "A rain tub.
We can save water in this!"

"Look! Lots of water!" said Bob.